"Once in his life a man ought to concentrate his mind upon the remembered earth. He ought to give himself up to a particular experience; to look at it from as many angles as he can, to wonder upon it, to dwell upon it.

"He ought to imagine he touches it with his hands at every season and listens to the sounds that are made upon it.

"He ought to imagine the creatures there and all the faintest motions of the wind. He ought to recollect the glare of the moon and the colours of the dawn and dusk."

N. Scott Momaday

The
PURE LAND
A Celebration of Wild Places

John Beatty

with 80 photographs

Thames and Hudson

For Jan

Title Page:
1   *Man directly in touch with nature: a*
solitary individual as meaningful in a
landscape as an isolated tree.

Printed and bound in Singapore by C.S. Graphics

Contents

Introduction	6	
Chapter One	19	Common Ground
Chapter Two	30	Priested Shores
Chapter Three	42	A Way out to Earth and Sky
Chapter Four	60	The Wasteland
Chapter Five	71	Gates of Eden
Chapter Six	85	The Wave Cry, the Wind Cry
Chapter Seven	98	Beautiful Vision

Introduction

*"I love this country passionately,
expanding to its wild immensity
as a flower opens in the sunshine."*

Hugh McDairmid

The Derbyshire moors are a sublime landscape of high heather plateaus and barren gritstone edges jutting to the West. This land has remained unchanged in the course of centuries buffeted by the wind and rain of industrial Northern England: a wild oasis of rocks and streams, of peat bogs and cotton grass, of uncertain shapes in the mist and the melancholy chirl of curlews.

I wander in these lovely hills, often in the wintertime with my collar turned up against the gale, my hands deep in my pockets, and I think of my friends in the city below, the traffic, the noise, the wet streets – and I think too of the Indian in the desert, who knows only his footprints in the bare earth and the arc of the sun in the heavens. I think of his reverence for nature, of the tenacity that enables him to live in the harshness of the wildest places.

Modern technology, especially in communications, has enabled us to travel widely on our planet, so that very few corners remain untouched. The imagination and aspirations of early travelers and explorers are where we look for the inspiration that may give us confidence to search beyond the boundaries of modern life and make our contact with nature. A personal exploration must take place before we can recognize and respond to the natural forces at work in the land, to feel the power and beauty of primal experiences.

As long as the wild land remains unchanged, we can all learn for ourselves the precision and complexity of the earth in harmony. If the land is altered in any way by our passage through it, then we are responsible for its inevitable destruction.

*"Tread softly, for this is holy ground.
It may be, could we look with seeing eyes,
This spot we stand on is Paradise."*

Christina Rossetti

2   *Kinder Downfall, in the hills of Derbyshire: a wild plateau of rocks and moors, no more than 2,000 feet above the city.*

3   *The unpeopled expanses of ocean, sand and seastacks: Cannon Beach, on the coast of Oregon.*

4   *The collared lizard, one of the creatures adapted to survive in the parched heat of the American desert.*

Overleaf:
5   *The life-giving element of water: the pool of Loch an Firbhallaich in the Cuillin Mountains of Skye, Scotland.*

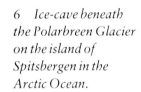

6   *Ice-cave beneath the Polarbreen Glacier on the island of Spitsbergen in the Arctic Ocean.*

7   *When the pack-ice breaks up in the arctic spring, newly opened leads become early feeding sites for many rare birds like this ivory gull, photographed at 78° north and -25°F.*

8 *In the Mont Blanc massif, the Aiguille de Blatière and the Aiguille de Charmoz, Chamonix, after a storm.*

Overleaf:
9 *The dawning of day on the Bens of Connemara, County Galway, Ireland: quietness, solitude, wonder are all joined here.*

Chapter One
Common Ground

The intricate balance of constant change and polarity in nature is manifest all about us in the physics of life. The pulse and the interval, the poles of a magnet, the firm and the yielding, the male and the female, the sunny and the shady. However we may interpret these gentle shifts and changes, they are most clearly seen in the actions and behaviour of creatures in the wild and their interrelationships with temporal and seasonal cycles. As our knowledge increases of their complex patterns, and of climate, soils, water, plants and man himself, we are left to wonder at the profound order of our small planet when nature is truly at peace.

The inevitable alteration of night and day is mirrored in the rhythmic activity of abounding life. Some creatures thrive in the light, some in the darkness. They thrive in the same habitat, the same physical space, but at different times.

The earth's creatures move through the intimate cycles of birth, reproduction and death, and at the same time the very structure of the environment in which they live is ever-changing. Water flows from mountain to ocean, evaporates, condenses and falls as rain in the mountains that in turn feed the oceans. Fire created the sources of life: the burning sun, the molten core of the earth. It enables us to live, without it we would die. From the earth we grew, to the earth we return.

10   *The rising of the moon at sunset on Malham Moor, Yorkshire.*

Overleaf:

11-13   *The eternal round of nature: a gray squirrel busy collecting food in the English oakwood; aspen leaves in autumn reflect the rhythms of nature; sulfur-tuft toadstools flourish in the damp forests of Derbyshire.*

14   *The loneliness of a woodland swamp in New Hampshire.*

18

15 *The moonlit waters of Lochmaddy in Uist, Outer Hebrides, seem to express the fragility and harmony of elemental nature.*

22

16   A gannet flying out to sea from one of the crowded seabird colonies of Bass Rock on the Solway Firth, Scotland.

17, 18   Water flowing through the frozen streambed at Devil's Kitchen, Cwm Idwal, in North Wales; and a detail of Thunder River careering through Grand Canyon.

19 *A view of the Oregon coast near Hug Point; in the foreground is a tangle of kelp seaweed.*

20 Driftwood carved by water and sand, and bleached by the sun at York Bay in the Falkland Islands.

28

Chapter Two
Priested Shores

Under lowering skies, the Hebridean islands of Scotland appear as Britain's last frontier – bleak, inhospitable and windswept, submerged in the cold Atlantic. Miles of shell sand beaches stretch alongside the clear blue water, underlaid by mauve seaweed and sandy greens. There is salt on the wind and the air carries the cry of seabirds and surf.

The islands share a strange combination of mildness (for they lie in the warm North Atlantic drift, an offshoot from the Gulf Stream helped by the prevailing westerly wind) and stark bleakness when arctic air flows down from the north. Even out on some of the most exposed islands there are places where folds in the hills provide soil and shelter rich in flowers and trees. More common, though, are the naked islands of rock and heather, with small trees lying tightly against the ground, firm and low in the incessant wind.

Each of the islands is remarkably different and unique in character. One can sit among palm trees, azaleas and magnolias in a protected valley on Colonsay, or lean on the tearing wind in the Atlantic sand dunes of Uist, or climb along the ancient gabbro spine of the Cuillin Mountains of Skye.

21   *A rest for contemplation on the summit of Sgurr Dearg, in the Cuillins; the island of Rhum is in the background.*

Overleaf: 22   *Far out on a misty headland, you may walk in a henge of tall silent stones, as in the Ring of Brogar (Orkneys). The very stones and the spaces between them are filled with the testament of a wild and powerful ancient people.*

23 *The beach of Traigh na Brac on the west coast of Colonsay.*

24,25   *A rainbow at Bracadale, Skye. Above, a tiny Church of Scotland building in the same area.*

26   *The puffins waddle to the edge of a cliff, whizz out over the sea, and return with their beaks full of sand eels for their chicks.*

Overleaf:
27   *Water flowing off the moors of An Grianan, near Cape Wrath, Scotland.*

Chapter Three
A Way out to Earth and Sky

The mountain has always symbolized freedom, a way of being, a way of seeing. For some, the mountain experience is entirely physical; for others it is mystical. Our aim is not to escape from the world, but to replenish ourselves from weariness, to discover and to be acutely aware of a reality far from where we live; and then to turn back towards home illuminated and nourished by the experience.

Inwardly, the world of the rock-climber has changed little since Mummery climbed the Grepon in 1902. Outwardly, pressures have been exerted by the climbing community. Guidebooks and grading systems have come to affect our basic goals, our techniques and our choice of climbs by rigidly measuring our progress. This interrupts our real climbing experience – for rock is gentle, persuasive, and demands a detachment that enables the climber to enter a state where precision and grace define the world, where the bond between rock and climber becomes inseparable.

Climbing in mountains has to do with commitment, fluency, and unfettered joy. A way out to earth and sky; sacred and inviolate places for meditation and peace.

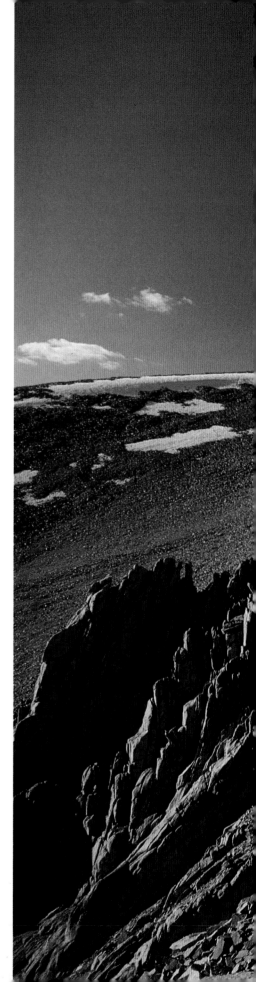

28   *On the summit of Mt. Whitney in the Sierras of California.*

Overleaf:
29   *The frontier ridge of Mt. Maudit in the Mont Blanc massif.*

30   *Winter gully climbing on the Black Ladders, Ysgolion Duon, the Carneddau Mountains, North Wales.*

31   *A dream climb, the South Ridge of the Aiguille Noire de Peuterey on the southeast face of Mont Blanc: a black sabre rising 13,000 feet to a precipitous summit.*

32 *Retreating from the Nose El Capitan, Yosemite, California.*

33, 34   The British rock-climber, Ron Fawcett, ascending the walls of Gordale Scar, Yorkshire.

35   The Old Man of
Hoy in the Orkneys of
Scotland, *a 400-foot
sandstone monolith
attached to the land by
a boulder causeway, is
one of Britain's
loneliest and finest
climbs.*

36   The Cuillins in winter offer the supreme mountain expedition that can be undertaken in Britain.

37   Ben Nevis by moonlight in winter. This Scottish peak, the highest in Britain, is the main centre of ice-climbing.

Overleaf:
38   Crossing to the Old Man of Storr, on the Easter spring tide.

39   *A chance to relax
after climbing the Old
Man of Storr,
Lochinver, northwest
Scotland.*

Chapter Four
The Wasteland

In the summer of 1888, the Norwegian biologist Fridtjof Nansen, with three fellow Norwegians and two Lapps, became the first man to cross the deserted inland ice wastes of Greenland. Almost a hundred years later, five colleagues and I joined to attempt to repeat Nansen's historic feat.

Immediately after we unloaded our supplies on a rock bluff and watched the boat that had brought us struggle back to the mouth of Sermilik Fjord, we were enveloped by wet heavy clouds that drifted in from the sea. When we were finally able to set out from the coastal tundra to the edge of the inland ice-cap – a distance of only 2½ miles – it took us three days because of our heavy supplies.

For twelve days after that we struggled with appalling loads on our backs. The bare ice was relentless; crevasses continuously blocked our passage forward. Days of heavy rain followed days of ice gales sweeping down from the inland sea. The stormy gusts inverted our tents twice, and on one day we managed to move camp only 400 meters.

The ascent was 9,000 feet over a distance of 200 miles. The freezing headwind made movement difficult and often impossible; on occasion we were blown totally adrift by several miles. Then one morning we awoke to the dull silence of abated weather. After the frenzy of so many hopeless days, we were surrounded by calm. Here at the highest and most central point of the Greenland ice-cap there was an inhospitable, frozen stillness to numb the senses. It drove us forward, over the last ethereal dome, to begin an imperceptible descent to the west coast nearly 200 miles on.

When the wind sprang up, it drove us along our route like autumn leaves; we were able to achieve daily records of 25 miles. The loads were becoming lighter as we used up our supplies. The sledge runners pointed downhill and homeward. We saw an airplane in the sky heading west. The real world was close at hand.

After forty-four days and some 400 miles of enormous exertion and struggle simply to keep alive, we rounded an ice-pond and saw before us pebbles and stones pitted into the ice leading away to the gray morranic debris of the ice-edge. We had left the ice behind us and were back in the world of rocks and grass and moss. But we felt that we had also left behind us the pure world.

40 *The start of the expedition: leaving the east coast.*

41,42   *On the Greenland ice-cap at 5,000 feet; sunrise at 1 a.m.
("The time will soon come/When we can rest./Our small crosses
will stand together/On the bright edge of the road."* Hermann
Hesse)

43 *The arctic phenomenon known as parhelion (mock sun, or "sun dog"), caused by the sun rising at dawn and seen through ice clouds. At this point our party was at an altitude of 8,000 feet and the temperature was −52°F.*

44,45   *A four-day storm; in spite of freezing headwind and blizzard, we marched on in conditions of zero visibility.*

46   *The sledges tended to sink in the soft surface of new snow. Everyone together had to pull them in order to keep moving.*

Overleaf:
47   *Descending to the west coast from the peak of the ice-cap, 120 miles to go – plain sailing with assistance from the wind.*

Chapter Five
Gates of Eden

Deep in the hidden chasms of the Grand Canyon, beneath the high plateau of the rim country, lies one of the most astonishing and impressive environments on earth. The titanic sculpturing of winds and rivers over millions of years has shaped a range of mountains 277 miles long, deep in a hole, with peaks and mesas rising to 5,000 feet. So curiously shaped are some of these peaks that early explorers called them sky-islands and -temples.

Hiking in the remote regions of the Canyon is a serious affair. Water only appears on the surface below the Red Walls, some 3,000 feet down from the rim. On this resurgence line are grottoes, slot gorges, pools, and terraces of unequalled beauty.

The Esplanade is one of these huge terraces, an expanse of bare, wind-eroded rock, carved into landscape that looks flat from a distance but is actually moulded into miniature gorges, boulder fields and gravel dunes; at its precipitous edge at the top of the Supai Red Walls there is a view even more breathtaking than that afforded from the rim.

A couple of hours' hike through searing heat leads to Thunder River, which provides in all that aridity an oasis of cotton trees, bamboo and willow along its sandy banks. Constant splashing from the bouldery river moistens thick clusters of maidenhair fern. Cushion mosses well with clear water. Up in the cliffs above the luxuriant swath of green, the river cascades in a fairytale waterfall. If the Garden of Eden existed, it was here in the upper reaches of Thunder River.

In 1869, Civil War veteran John Wesley Powell, accompanied by nine men, travelled down the Colorado River in small wooden boats, throughout the entire length of the Canyon. The Indians were afraid of the river. Navaho, Hopi and Ute all believed in an ancient flood that had inundated their ancestors, turning them into fish; they were also taught that the river had high waterfalls which eventually drained into a vast hole, the very heart of the earth, deep within the Canyon.

When Powell came to the end of his historic journey, he wrote: "Every waking hour passed in the Grand Canyon has been one of toil. . . . Now the danger is over, now the toil has ceased, now the gloom has disappeared, now the firmament is bounded only by the horizon. The river rolls by us in silent majesty; the quiet of the camp is sweet; our joy is ecstasy."

48   *The spectacular view from the Esplanade on the North Rim of Grand Canyon, looking down to the Dubendorf Rapids.*

Overleaf: 49   *The inner gorge as seen from the South Rim, one hour after sunset.*

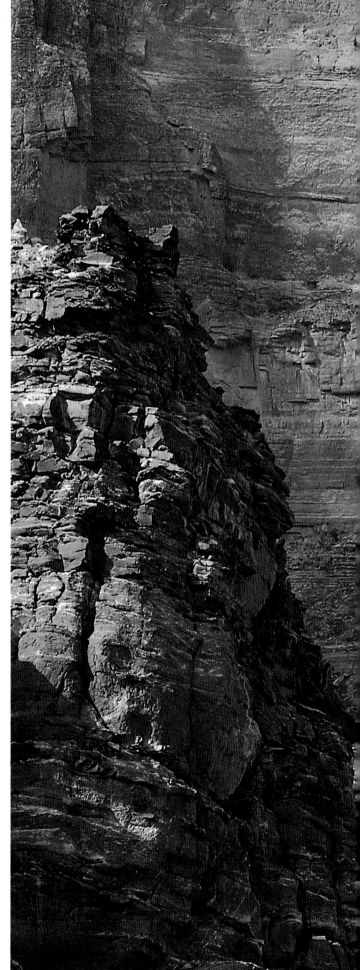

50   *A delicate blooming wildflower in the depths of the Canyon.*

51   *Spiderlets spinning webs in the spines of a barrel cactus.*

52   *The great barrier of the Supai Red Walls.*

Overleaf:
53   *Negotiating a slot-gorge in Tapeats Creek. Many times along the Creek, the gorge narrows to a keyhole, with long sections to be waded and wall climbs leading back to the wooded banks. In two miles of hiking, the Creek may have to be crossed fourteen times.*

54,55   *The Deer Creek Falls jet out of the travertine walls and form a pool of clear, cool water.*

Overleaf:

56   *Tapeats Cave: the entrance feels ancient with the dust of death. The low roof arches 60 feet across under the Red Walls above the Creek. A tortuous passage, twisting and narrowing, leads eventually to an enormous lake: a cool, hidden vault inside the desert, fed by snowmelt streams on the Kaibab Plateau 4,000 feet above.*

57   *Bathing in the tumultuous waters of Deer Creek.*

58   *Rock walls in the Canyon sculptured by water.*

Chapter Six

The Wave Cry, The Wind Cry

In 1772 Captain James Cook set sail for the Southern Ocean in quest of
Terra Australis Incognita, the hidden southern land. Although doubtful
of its existence, he steadfastly sailed through the huge seas of the
Roaring Forties until his little vessels were girded by flotillas of
glittering icebergs. The fogs and snowstorms and stiffening sails
frightened the crew. Cook decided to go no farther. He had seen the
cold eerie light of the pack ice "as if from beneath the sea." If there was a
continent beyond, Cook no longer cared.

After three summers he pulled his boats up on a rocky beach. He
described seals and penguins in their hundreds crowding the foreshore.
South Georgia had been discovered. Cook called it a "savage and
horrible country, with wild rocks, lofty summits lost in cloud and vallies
buried in ever-lasting snow. Not a tree, not a shrub was to be seen, no
not even big enough to make a toothpick."

In 1971 I was able to join a research ship carrying out assignments in
Antarctica. My first stop was the Falkland Islands; and from there the
ship travelled out towards Halley Bay at 82° south. It was a strange
journey for our little boat, nosing through the desert pack of the
Weddell Sea to a stark planet as distant from home as I ever wished to be
– to an unholy birthplace where, under a greying sky, giant icebergs
were carving from the cliffs. On a dim-lit ocean they would float to
more northern waters to be polished like pebbles in a raging sea.

With a team under Dr Brian Storry, I participated in a sledging
journey of some 200 miles to collect specimens of rock from the coastal
mountains of Adelaide Island. The oppression of winter in the Antarctic
is unsettling to think about, not so much because of the cold as the iron
indifference and terrible weight of darkness.

And yet, when I eventually left for home again I was overwhelmed by
a sense of loss. In due course the sea would cease to move, Antarctica
would grow dark again and strange and silent. Only the moon would
glow over the empty ice. For four months, time would stand cold and
still, until spring broke again with the advent of a new sun and the tide
swelled beneath the ice-pack.

59   The Royal Research Ship John Biscoe *searching for open leads in the summer
pack-ice of De Gerlache Straits, in the Antarctic Peninsula. In the background are the
huge walls of Mt. Français, Anvers Island.*

60,61   *The Peri-Antarctic islands are havens of highly adapted wildlife, such as these chinstrap penguins. Above, a fur seal cow and suckling pup; South Georgia in midsummer.*

Overleaf:
62   *Cumberland Bay in South Georgia. In the background are the highest peaks of the Alledice Mountains, Mt. Paget and Mt. Nordensköld.*

63 *A sooty albatross in South Georgia.*

64 *Icebergs in the still waters off the west coast of Adelaide Island.*

65   An ice-strengthened ketch from Europe sailing in
Cumberland Bay, South Georgia.

66   Two gentou penguins courting, with the wall peaks of
Wienke Island in the background.

67   A rest stop while sledging with a dog team on the frozen sea.
Jenny Island is in the background.

Overleaf:
68   Tidal icicles, formed by the receding tide and caught by the
midnight sun.

69   *An aerial view of the Antarctic Peninsula in early summer evening light.*

Chapter Seven
Beautiful Vision

Industrialized man is a cause of deadly pollution, but curiously shrinks from taking drastic corrective action. Whole forests in Europe are dying as the normal soil nutrients are washed away and replaced by a lethal cocktail of toxic metals. In many lakes fish are suffocating, their gills becoming clogged with aluminium hydroxide.

Our responsibility to look after our earth is ultimately a matter of relationships, first between man and nature, and then between man and man. The comparatively modern idea that we inhabit a "biosphere," in which all the earth's forms are inextricably connected, is now widely understood and accepted. Nevertheless, the present-day destruction of the rain forest, probably the most threatened single habitat on earth, involves a rate of extinction of life of perhaps one species per day.

Man needs to maintain an equilibrium in his own biosphere. We need green plants, water and stability in the complicated web of life. We need to conserve and protect natural areas of our earth, so that our children can go into the wilderness unfettered, to laugh and dance and run free close to their desire and imagination, holding fast to a sacred inheritance.

70   *Omey Island, County Galway, one of the most westerly points of the European continent.*

71 *The peak of Stob Dearg near Glencoe, Scotland, in early spring.*

72,73 *Sycamore leaf litter in an English forest; and the tree frog, which is mainly found in the moist temperate woodlands of America.*

74 *The lonely winter woodcutter, Staffordshire.*

75 Woods in the Pennine Range, England, affected by acid rain: sulfuric and nitric acids caused by the chemical reaction with the atmosphere of the sulfur dioxide and nitrogen oxides discharged in the burning of fossil fuels.

76 Mono Lake in northern California, whose placid surface rises and falls drastically as the water requirement of Los Angeles alters. The barren shoreline is struggling to keep in balance, and the salinity of the water fluctuates so radically that the life in the lake and the creatures that feed from it are all threatened.

Overleaf:
77 Sandpipers off the coast of Oregon.

78   On the east coast
of Spitsbergen in
March, 10 p.m. with
the temperature at
−40°F.

79 . . . that our
children may run
free among the
receding waves of the
ocean . . .

80   A fire of driftwood on a beach called Sandwood Bay, west coast of Scotland.

"Over all hung the breathless hush of evening.
One heard it circle the world like a lapping tide,
The wave beat of the sea of beauty.
We began to understand, a little less darkly,
What it might mean to inherit the Earth."

W. H. Murray